PAPER PIECING
PATTERNS

BONNIE K. BROWNING

American Quilter's Society
P. O. Box 3290 • Paducah, KY 42002-3290
FAX: 502-898-8890 *http://www.AQSquilt.com*

Located in Paducah, Kentucky, the American Quilter's Society (AQS) is dedicated to promoting the accomplishments of today's quilters. Through its publications and events, AQS strives to honor today's quiltmakers and their work and to inspire future creativity and innovation in quiltmaking.

TECHNICAL EDITOR: BARBARA SMITH
BOOK DESIGN/ILLUSTRATIONS: ANGELA SCHADE
COVER DESIGN: MICHAEL BUCKINGHAM
PHOTOGRAPHY: CHARLES R. LYNCH

Library of Congress Cataloging-in-Publication Data
Browning, Bonnie K.
    Paper Piecing Patterns / Bonnie K. Browning
                    p.   cm.
    ISBN 1-57432-737-2
    1. Patchwork--Patterns.   2. Patchwork quilts.
                            I. Paper Piecing Patterns.
TT   .C   1999
746.   Applied for
                                        CIP

Additional copies of this book may be ordered from the American Quilter's Society, PO Box 3290, Paducah, KY 42002-3290 @ $14.95. Add $2.00 for postage and handling.

Printed in the U.S.A. by Image Graphics, Paducah, KY

DEDICATION

To all those who have been involved in the evolution of the sewing machine and to those who developed techniques for making quilts by machine, because your efforts make it possible for quilters to use modern technology and updated methods to sew our quilts.

ACKNOWLEDGMENTS

Special thanks to:

Karen Burrier, who asked me to stitch a block for her paper-pieced quilt in the early 1980s. It was my introduction to paper piecing.

Mary Sowell and Joyce Rinella for helping sew blocks.

My friends, Phyllis Miller, Marie Salazar, and Ruth Ann Thompson, who share ideas, and encourage me to get some stitching done. Our retreats always energize me.

Meredith Schroeder and all the staff at the American Quilter's Society for publishing this book; Angela Schade for design and layout, Michael Buckingham for the cover, and Charles R. Lynch for the photography.

Patterns appear on inside front cover and inside back cover.

TABLE OF CONTENTS

INTRODUCTION 5

SUPPLIES 6

FOUNDATIONS 6
     Materials
     Marking Paper Patterns

FABRICS 7
     Choosing Fabrics
     Grain Lines
     Cutting Fabric

SETTING UP YOUR SEWING SPACE 8
     Getting Ready
     Sewing Machine

SEWING BLOCKS STEP-BY-STEP 9

PATTERNS 12

INDEX 32

Tree 2, Cabin, Tree 1, Barn, Tree 3

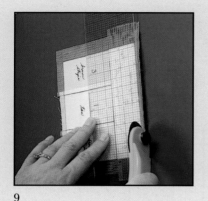
9

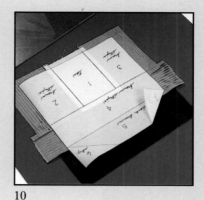
10

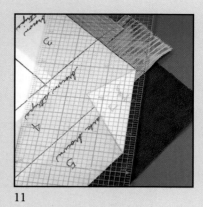
11

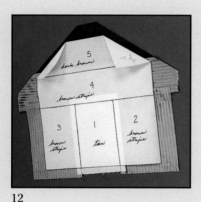
12

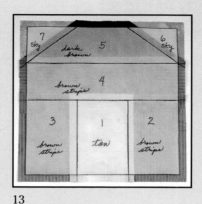
13

14

15

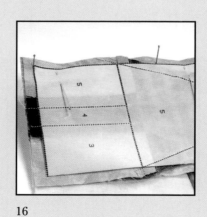
16

Tips
•Seam allowances are trimmed to ¼" on each piece as it is sewn and on the outside edges of the block when it is completed.
•Any time you sew a very light fabric to a dark fabric, be sure to check the seam allowance from the fabric side of the block; often you will need to trim the seam allowance a little more because the dark fabric shadows through the light fabric.
•The printed side of the pattern is the back side of the block.

Step 9: Fold the paper back and trim the seam allowance ¼" beyond the seam line.

Step 10: Sometimes it is easier to place a piece on an angle if you trim the seam allowance before positioning the fabric. Fold the paper back on the stitching line.

Step 11: Trim the fabric of the last piece added to ¼" beyond the folded edge. Now you have the correct angle.

Step 12: Trim both angles in preparation for adding the corner triangles.

Step 13: Continue adding pieces in order until the paper foundation is covered.

Step 14: The finished block.

Step 15: To join units or sections of a block together or to join blocks, place a positioning pin in each corner of the blocks, pulling the two pieces together.

Step 16: Insert another pin beside the positioning pin. Sew blocks together along the paper edge. Press seam allowance open to reduce bulk. When the quilt has been completed, remove the paper foundation. Use a pin to lift the paper away from the fabric and tear it carefully away from the seams. If you have sewn into the paper, a pair of tweezers will help remove those small bits.

BARN

Finished size: 6" x 6"
Split foundation

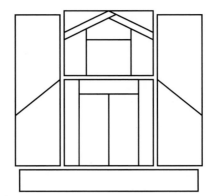

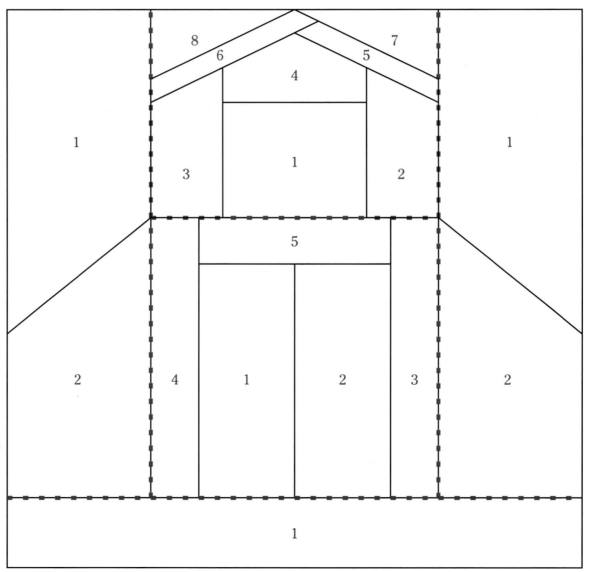

Paper Piecing Patterns – Bonnie K. Browning

CABIN

Finished size: 6" x 6"
Single block

```
        6          5          7

                   4

        2          1          3
```

HOUSE

Finished size: 6" x 6"
Single block

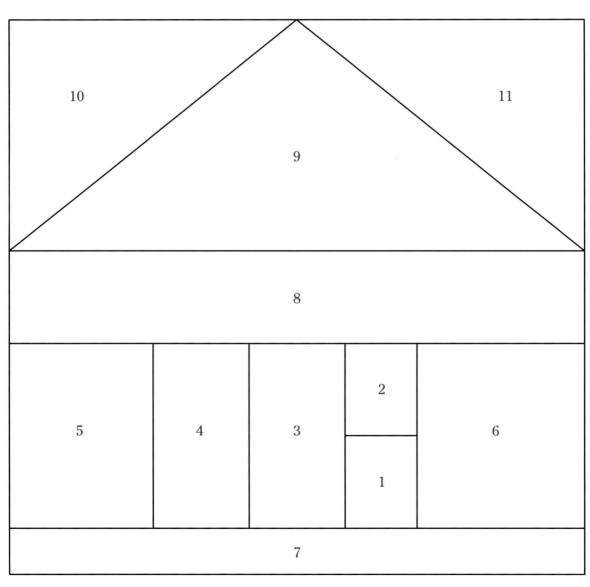

SQUIRREL EATING CORN

Finished size: 6" x 6"
Split foundation

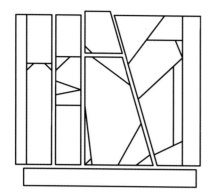

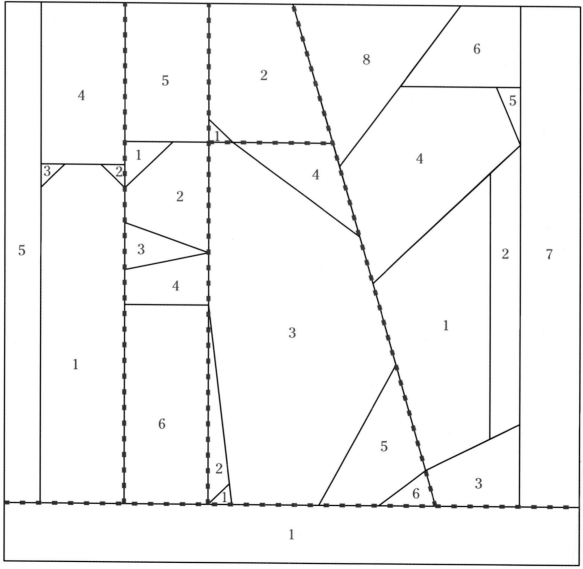

Finished size: 6" x 6"
Split foundation

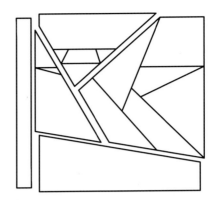

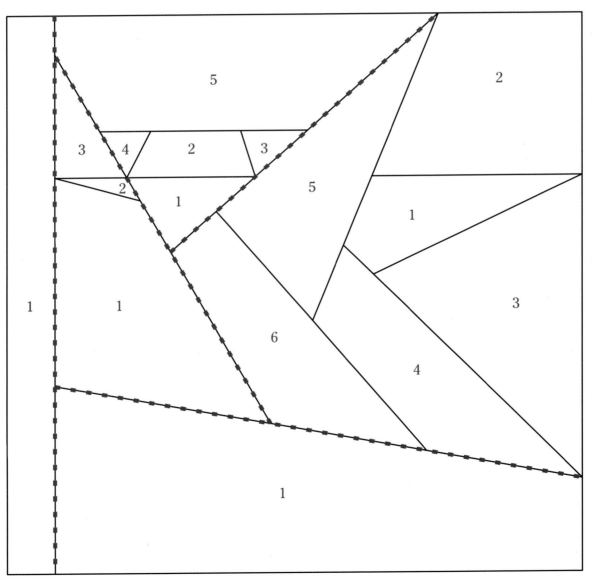

Paper Piecing Patterns – Bonnie K. Browning

TREE 1

Finished size: 6" x 6"
Single block

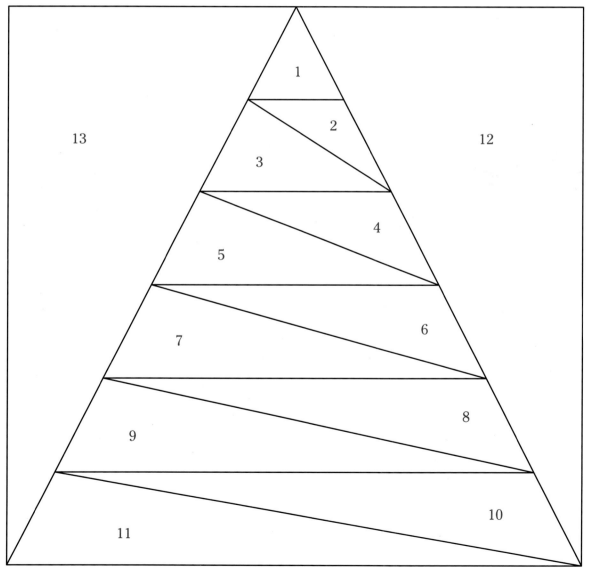

TREE 2

Finished size: 3" x 6"
Single block

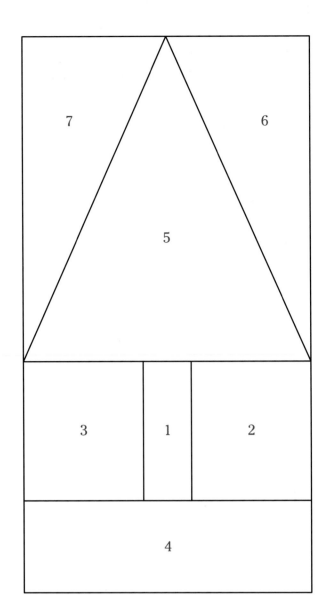

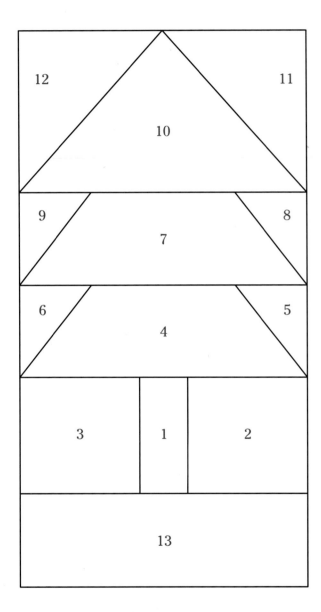

TREE 3

Finished size: 3" x 6"
Single block

SNOWBALL VARIATION

Finished size: 6" x 6"
Single block

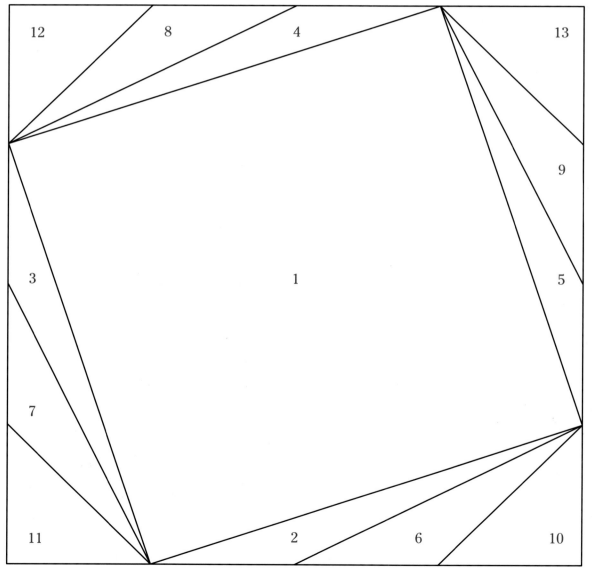

PINEAPPLE

Finished size: 6" x 6"
Single block

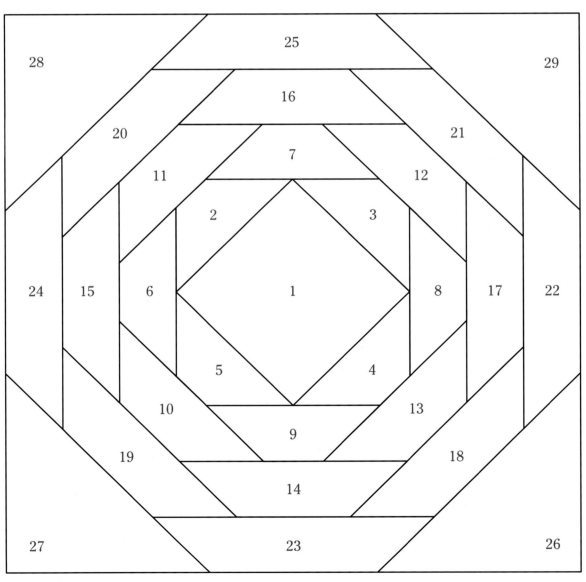

Paper Piecing Patterns – Bonnie K. Browning

LOG CABIN
COURTHOUSE STEPS

Finished size: 6" x 6"
Single block

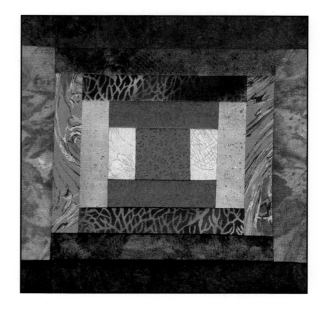

					15					
					10					
					6					
					3					
16	12	8	4		1		5	9	13	17
					2					
					7					
					11					
					14					

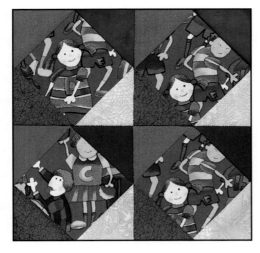

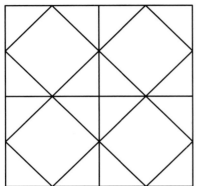

DIAMOND IN A SQUARE

Finished size: 6" x 6"
Quarter block: Make four of pattern

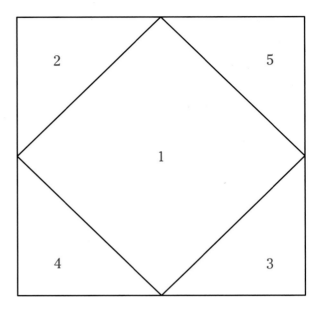

DOUBLE PINWHEEL WHIRLS

Finished size: 6" x 6"
Quarter block: Make four of pattern

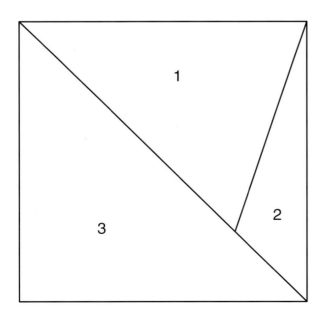

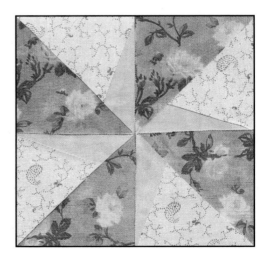

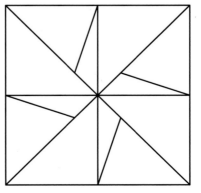

JOB'S TROUBLES

Finished size: 8" x 8"
Quarter block: Make four of pattern

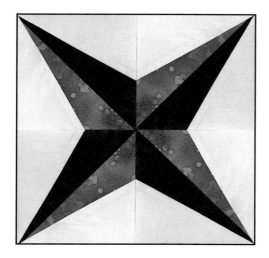

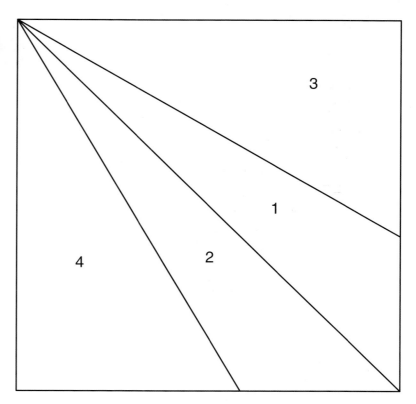

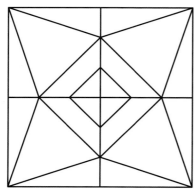

3-D

Finished size: 6" x 6"
Quarter block: Make four of pattern

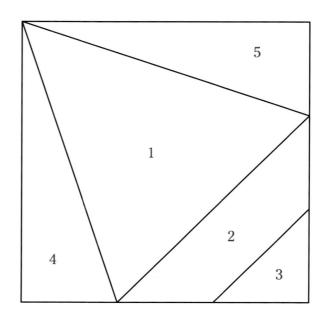

ROSE

Finished size: 6" x 6"
Single block

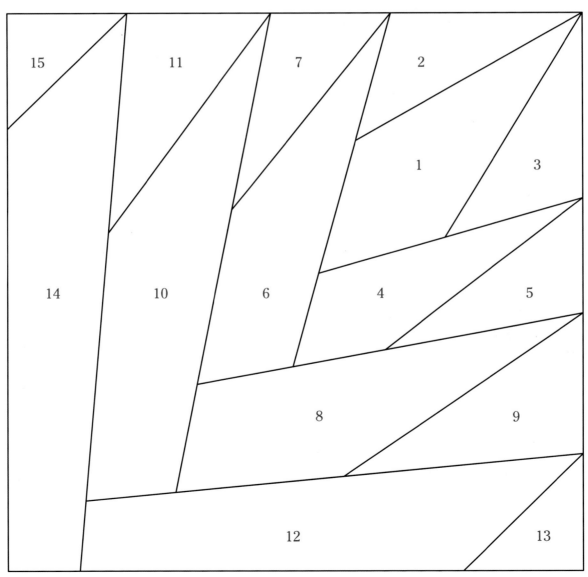

Paper Piecing Patterns – Bonnie K. Browning

DAFFODIL

Finished size: 6" x 6"
Single block with pre-sewn units #5 and #6

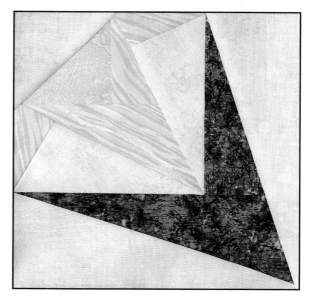

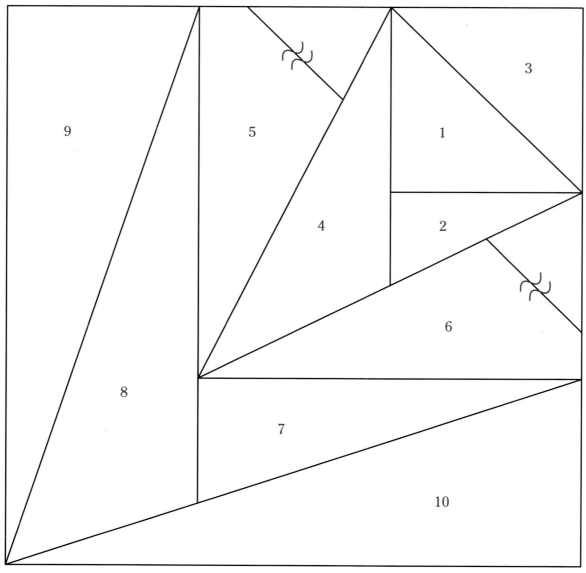

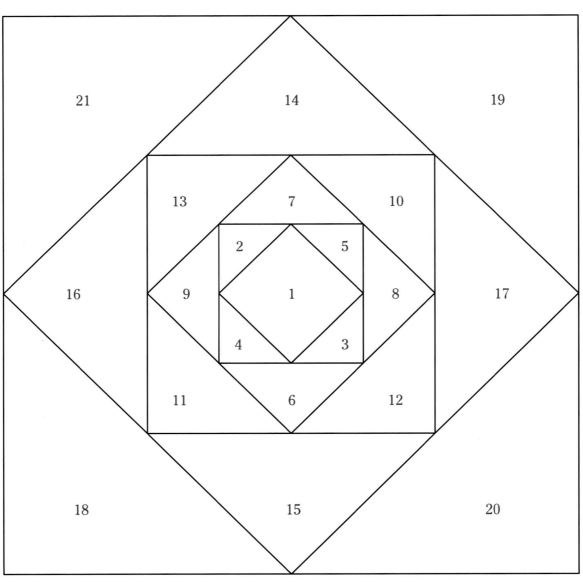

PALM LEAF

Finished size: 6" x 6"
Split foundation

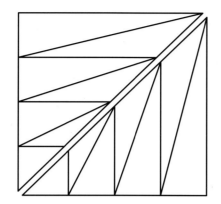

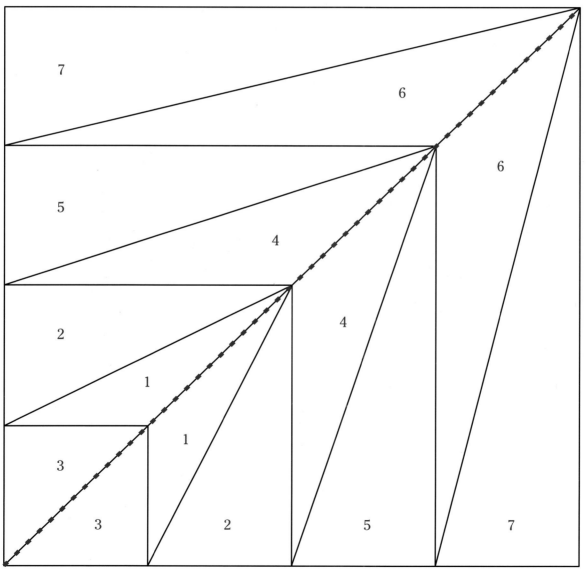

CROSSED CANOES

Finished size: 6" x 6"
Quarter block: Make four of pattern

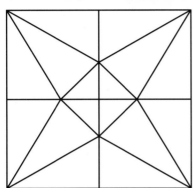

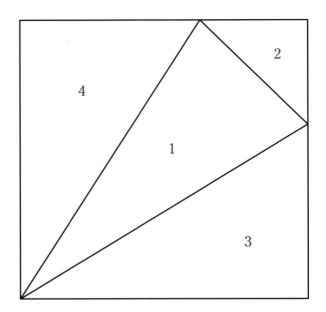

STAR & SQUARE

Finished size: 6" x 6"
Quarter block: Make four of pattern

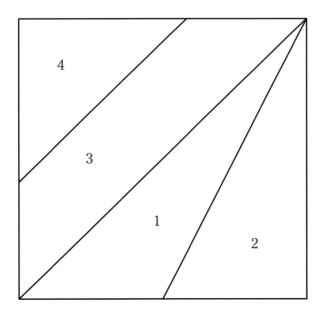

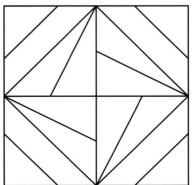

SHOOTING STARS

Finished size: 12" x 12"
Quarter block: Make sixteen of pattern

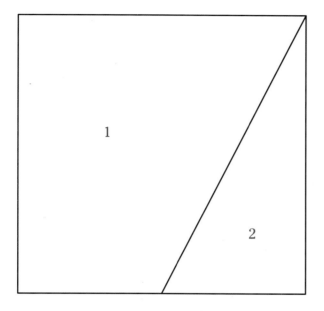

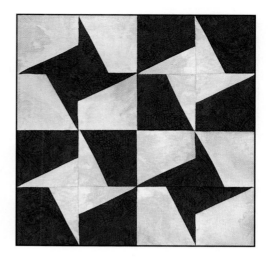

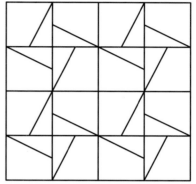

SHOOTING STAR

Finished size: 8" x 8"
Quarter block: Make four of pattern

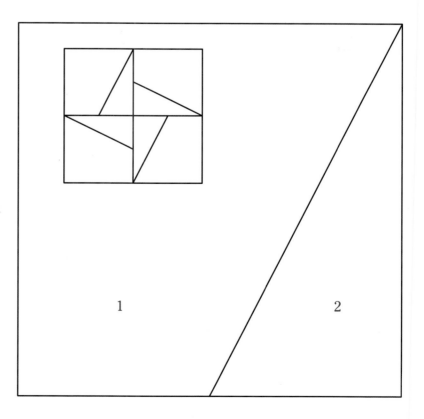

AIRPLANE

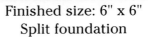

Finished size: 6" x 6"
Split foundation

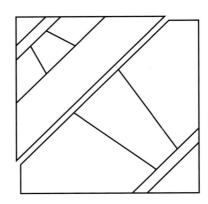

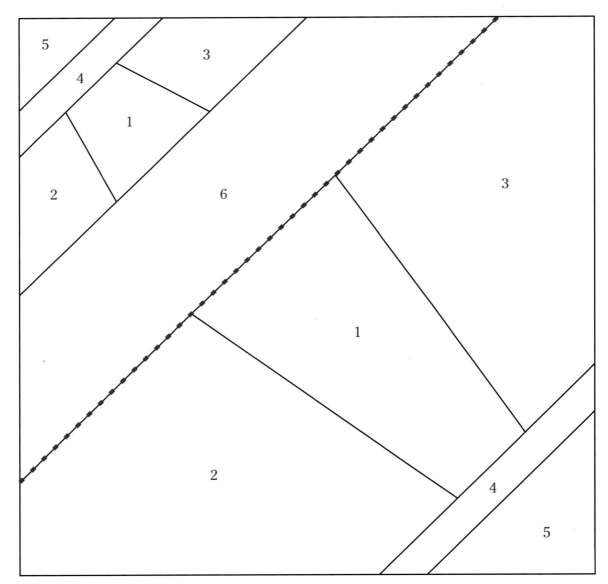

Paper Piecing Patterns – Bonnie K. Browning

SAILBOAT

Finished size: 6" x 6"
Single block

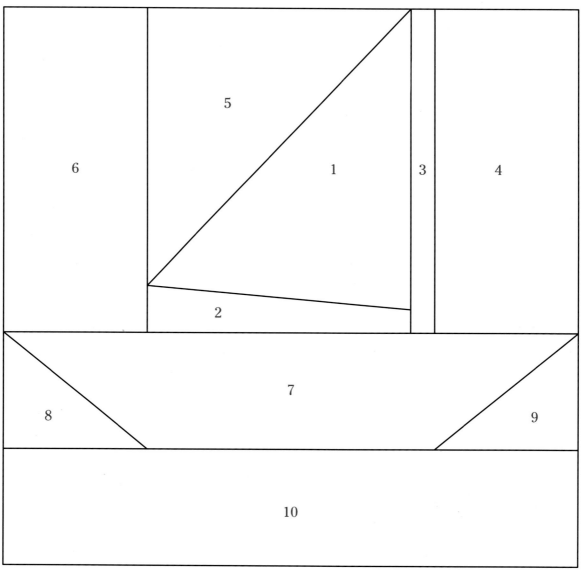

INDEX

Airplane 30
Barn 12
Cabin 13
Chocolate Cake . . . . .inside back cover
Choosing Fabrics 7
Coffee Cup . . . . .inside back cover
Coffee Pot . . . . .inside back cover
Cupcake . . . . .inside front cover
Crossed Canoes 28
Cutting Fabric .8
Daffodil 25
Diamond in a Square 22
Double Pinwheel Whirls 22
Grain Lines 7
House 14
Hummingbird .16
Job's Troubles .23
Log Cabin – Courthouse Steps 21
Marking Paper Patterns 6
Materials 6

Mosaic Rose 26
Palm Leaf 27
Pineapple 20
Rose 24
Shooting Stars (3-inch) 29
Shooting Star (4-inch) 29
Sailboat 31
Setting Up Your Sewing Space 8
Sewing Blocks Step-by-Step 9
Signature Heart (photo only) 1
Snowball Variation 19
Squirrel Eating Corn 15
Star & Square .28
Supplies 6
Tea Cup . . . . .inside front cover
Teapot . . . . .inside front cover
Tree 1 17
Tree 2 18
Tree 3 18
3-D 23

MORE BOOKS BY BONNIE K. BROWNING

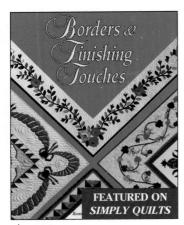